Mind blowing magic 2

Street magic

Contents

Street magic

Street magic is great it is amazingly good and can be performed anywhere with normal props. It is made up of two types of magic close up magic and impromptu magic. Impromptu magic is when you pretend things have gone wrong which distracts the spectators so you can do many wondrous things while they are not looking. Close up magic is one of the most amazing types because they never take their eyes off you but you still do it.

Samuel Innes

Author

Stopping your pulse

Effect the pulse is felt and is normal then after some hard concentration the magician stops their pulse.

Method: this is harmless and can be performed by anyone. First of all find your pulse you can do this by putting two fingers together. Place them either on your wrist. When you feel a steady ticking rhythm then you have found it. Simply squeeze a piece of paper into a ball. Then put it under your armpit and squeeze hard. This stops a major artery in your body but it is harmless. Then get a spectator to check your pulse and it should slow down and disappear. This will not work on your neck though you could try it.

Coin through table

Effect: a coin is shown and it goes straight through a solid table and is examined.

Method: before the trick you need to hide an identical coin in one hand. Show the audience the coin (not the hidden one) then place it between your index and thumb. Squeeze hard then let the coin shoot of in one direction. Make sure there is a newspaper nearby for it to slide under. Cover this action with the rest of your fingers. Pretend that you are taking the coin out from under the table with the hand that has the hidden coin in. This effect is amazing and can be performed many places.

Prediction paper

Effect: the magician asks some questions on the spectator and then the magician predicts them on the piece of paper. The paper is then opened to find the correct prediction every time.

Method: have a pack of cards and check the top card. Now ask a question like how many cups of tea have you had today. Then write down the name of the card that you just looked at and write 4 on the back. Place the answer under a bowl folded up. Ask the answer to the previous question and write it down. Say this is so they don't cheat because some people say this when actually this was the answer. Ask another question but write the answer to the first question and a 1 on the back. And do this again and write the answer to the second question. This time do the card trick: the twist and write the answer to the third question. All of the answers to the questions should be asked after the question is asked then you can copy them down. This time open the bowl and open up the predictions in number order. Watch as the amazement grows for a grand finale of their card. You can find the card trick: the twist in mind blowing magic. Mind blowing magic is the first in the series.

Coin through card

Effect: a coin is shown and examined; a card is shown. The coin is passed back and then the coin goes straight through the card.

Method: before the trick you need to cut a slit in the top of the card you want to use. Show them the coin and the card and maybe get the coin signed. Fold the card in half so the slit is closest to you. Get the coin and put it between the two half's and give it a magical wave. Though this will not work and then you say that you will try again. This time put the coin in the two half's and show them that. But put it through the slit and let the majority of the coin be on the outside. After that focus on the coin held up by your thumb then let it fall through.

Coin tear

Effect: a coin is shown then the magician rips it into shreds.

Method: to prepare for this trick you will need any silver coin and some foil. What you need to do is get the foil and put it over the coin. Push down hard so you get a print on the foil of the coin. Use a knife or get a grownup to help you cut of the excess foil. Show the fake coin and place it in a folded piece of paper being careful not to show the other side. Rip up the paper to show that the coin has completely vanished.

This trick is good because you have nothing left for them to inspect.

Cups and balls

Effect: a cup is placed down and a marble is placed on top of it. Another cup is placed on that then another. Then the magician gives it a tap and it penetrates the cup. This keeps going with more and more adding to the mix.

Method: all you need is four identical marbles and three non see-through cups. Lay out the three cups and under the one in the middle put a marble, you are now ready to start. Put the other three in front of each cup. Take a marble and put it on top of the cup in the middle. Place the other cups staking up on top of it and give the top one a tap. Lift off all three at once to show a marble underneath the cups and put them behind the marble. Take the cups off but when it comes to the second. Lean the tower over so the marble is in that cup then put it in the middle covering the marble. Then do the same and again lift them off and put them behind and so on.

Levitation

Effect: a magician says they'll try something then they concentrate hard then they slowly lift off the ground.

Method: Stand with your feet close together and say you will try something. Lift one foot off the ground and go on your toes on the other foot. This need to be viewed from where the lifted foot is at a 45° angle and the raised heel of the other foot is also visible from a 45° angle. When you land bend your legs a lot to exaggerate your height and fall. This if done well is absolutely amazing but can only be performed from this angle.

Appearing and disappearing pencil

Effect: a pencil is shown and then the magician shakes their hand and it has gone. They then shake their hand again and it reappears.

Method: before the trick put the very tip of a small pencil between your thumb and the lower side of your index finger. Make it not visible from the front and look natural. When you shake your hand get the two middle fingers and bend them back to get the pencil. So quickly reach round and grab the centre of the pencil. You can then let people examine it then make it disappear and appear again. Try to let your hand flow from the shake so if you shake it backwards and then forwards use that energy to follow your hand behind.

Cup through table

Effect: a coin is shown and a cup is placed over it a piece of paper is placed over the cup. He then tries to make the coin disappear and fails. So he tries again and this time he closes his eyes and pushed down on cup it goes right through the table. Then he takes it out from the bottom of the table.

Method: the first time you attempt it goes wrong on purpose. All you need is a coin a cup and some paper. The first time just try hard to do anything, it doesn't matter. lift it off to see if the coin has disappeared. Secretly drop the cup onto your lap then replace the paper on top of the coin. The paper should hold the shape of the cup if you pressed down hard enough. Now slowly start to push down and try and make I look hard. With the other hand grab the cup and remove it from under the table

Pencil through hand

Effect: a pencil is shown and the magician lifts the pencil up and slams it into their hand and instead of going through his hand it disappears.

Method: no preparation is needed though practise is still vital. When you lift the pencil up tuck it behind your ear. When you slam it down do this quickly so the pencil is hidden. No you can either make it so that it went wrong. Or you could clench your hand in a fist so that vanes stick out you could call these the pencil. You could then make it reappear or come out of your arm.

Levitating egg box

Effect: an egg box is shown and then it is let go of. It floats in the air then the magician catches it again.

Method: this is great if you can get the end right. All you need is an egg box and something long like a wooden spoon or flute cleaner. On the egg box, there is a hole where you would close it. Stick your stick into that hole and put the other end under your armpit. Make sure the spectators are viewing it from straight ahead. Let go of the egg box and pretend to focus hard on the box. Act like you can't take it much longer and grab the box. At this point drop the stick unnoticeably and bow.

Levitating cup

Effect: a cup is shown then held slowly but surely it moves away from their grasp, then they go to catch it.

Method: there are two ways you can do this the first way is more affective but requires a polystyrene cup. The second way needs any cup but sometimes makes noises. For the first way the cup needs a hole in the back. When the hole is created stick your thumb into it a very little bit but enough to hold it steadily. For the less effective way make a loop of sellotape and stick your thumb to that. In both cases you perform the same way. Hold onto the cup and slowly move the thumb attached forward and the rest of the hand stays in the same place. Also the other hand stays in the same place. Only hold the cup in the air for about 1 second. Then jolt forward and grab it.

Book test

Effect: two books are shown and the spectator chooses one. The spectator then chooses a page at random the first word on that page. The magician then correctly predicts the first word or even the sentence.

Method: before the trick you need to remember the first word of any page and either book and remember it all through the trick. Get them to point at one book if it is the book that you remembered the word in then let them have it. However if it is not the book then say that you get the book that they are pointing to. Flick through the book that you are holding and tell them to put their finger in. When they put their finger in then instead of saying that page number, say the page number of the word you remembered. Then start thinking of qualities that that word has and then tell them the word and watch them be amazed.

Coin through bottle 2

Effect: a coin is shown then put on top of a bottle and the bottle is hit with a pack of cards and the coin is in the bottle.

Method: to prepare for this trick put a piece of double sided sticky tape on the bottom of the pack of cards. Also put it on the lid of the bottle and stick one coin under there. Get an identical coin to the one under the lid. Place the coin on the bottle top and put the pack of cards on the coin. Remember that the pack of cards is picking up the coin so hide it. Lift the bottle up with the cards still on top and slam it on the table. The coin should fall from the bottle top and remember to hide the coin from view.

Disappearing pen 2

Effect: a pen is shown and held, and then slowly the hands of the magician close in until the pen has disappeared.

Method: sit at a table and place the pen lying between two hands. Then close the finger in front of the pen so it is not visible. Drop the pen on to your lap and look like it is still there by being natural. Slowly close the palms of your hands and rub them together and it has gone.

Toothpick penetration

Effect: two toothpicks are shown then the magician links them together and apart then together they are then examined.

Method: break the ends off the toothpicks and squeeze hard so when you remove the toothpicks there are little dips. In front of the mirror practise the toothpick only sticking to one finger. So you can make your fingers wider and the toothpick will still stay on one finger. Also practise the width of your finger covering the gap making it look like the toothpick is still on both fingers. When it comes to performance hold both the toothpicks and make sure they are on both fingers. Then when you come to penetrate swing your hand back then and when you get close quickly open and close the gap of one hand enough for it to link in.

Transporting coin

Effect: four coins are shown and four cards then the coins are laid down and then the cards on top. Then he proves that there is only one under each card then he puts the cards down and then up and there is two under on and none under the other. And on and on then on the last one he doesn't touch the cards and they transport.

Method: when you are lying out the coins make sure the table has a cloth over it. When it comes to put the cards on hold them as if you were holding a cylinder. So the four fingers are covering under the card. Place one card over the first coin but with your thumb push it against the four fingers and slide it over to the second coin leaving the card on top of nothing and be unnoticed. Place the card over the two coins and go over to the third then fourth normally. Pick up the third and the second but push until one of the coins hits your thumb and lift up the card. Make the coin is behind the card. Show then that there is one under each card. Go down and let go of the coin and pick up the one coin card which is the third card. So there appears to be two under one card and zero under the other. Remove the card covering the two coins and then put the card that the coin is behind on the two make three but don't show it. Then again pick up the fourth and show there is one under one and two under the other. Then drop one coin and pick up the other to show zero beneath one card and three under the other. Then remove the card covering the three and replace it with the card with the coin on the back. Now this time do it without touching the coins and get the spectator to lift off both cards. Make sure when you let go of the coins when you are putting the card down that the coin doesn't clink on any other coin.

Rising cloth

Effect: a cloth is shown and laid down then slowly and mysteriously it rises and then slowly drops.

Method: Hold up the cloth and with the thumb of you right hand hold onto a fork out of sight behind the cloth. As you lay it down try and not let the fork make a sound as it hits the table. Hold your hand above where the prongs are (right in the centre.) Slowly push on the other end with your elbow and it should rise up in the middle. Lower it down taking care to mask any sound made with patter. Then as you take it off to be examined drop the fork onto your lap and let it be examined.

Cut and restored string

Effect: a piece of string is shown and fed into a straw. The straw is cut and then the string is taken out in one piece.

Method: before the trick cut a little slit in the straw enough for the string to go through. Make sure the string is a thread the same colour as your clothes. Now put the thread in the straw and bend the straw. Pull hard on each end so the thread is now outside the straw and taking a short cut because of the slit. Cut at the top of the bend and hold the pieces together. Now let the string go back into the Brocken straw. And pull one end of the string out, it is all in one piece.

Tightrope walker

Effect: two pieces of string are shown and then put in the magicians hand he holds them and then they become one.

Method: before the trick, get a piece of string and make sure it is the one were the string is twisted. In the middle untwist about three centimetres of the string. You should now have two bits of the string hanging out. Get one of them and twist the bit hanging out and do that with the other one too. There should be a crazy bit in the middle were all the bits meet. Cover this with your hand so it looks like two pieces of string. Now put the made up ends of the two pieces of string in your hand and clench it into a fist. Get spectators to pull at each end of the real string and it will become one string again. Do not use the same string more than twice as it becomes frayed.

Pencil up nose

Effect: a pencil is shown and then put to the nose and then slowly it goes up their nose then slowly it comes back out again.

Method: This requires no preparation but a lot of practice. Get your two first fingers and cover the wooden bit so none of it is visible. Then with the other hand slowly let the hand go up and up giving the illusion that it is going up his nose. Make sure there are no designs on the pen or any words. Also make sure that the rest of the pencil is out of view.

The double dot paper

Effect: three cards are shown and written on, the spectator chooses one of the cards and the magician guesses what is on the other side.

Method: Get three pieces of card and in view of the spectator draw one dot on one side of one of them. With another card draw a dot on both sides of the paper. Then with another do not draw anything on it. Now get the spectator to put all the cards behind his back and choose one. Make sure to not let either you or him see the bottom. Now place it on the table and say you will guess what is on the other side. Let's say there was a dot on the top then say there was a dot on the bottom. If there was nothing on the top say there is nothing on the bottom. You are not guaranteed to get it right but it is a chance of ⅔.

Inside my eyes

Effect: a pack is shown and flicked through, the spectator memorises a card the magician concentrates deeply and tells the spectator their card.

Method: Remember the top card; this should be the card they memorise. Tell them to memorise a card and that it is not the back card. So flick through and at the first bit flick so fast that they cannot memorise any cards. At the last card slow down so they can remember it. Now from this there are many things you can do.

Knife effect

Effect: the spectator puts a knife in anywhere in the deck. The magician gives them the pack to memorise. Then they shuffle the pack and the magician tells them there card

Method: you will need a shiny knife for this trick and a pack of cards. Ask them to stick the knife in anywhere and give the pack to you. Now twist the knife so the top pack is raising and that you get a clear refection of the card. After that tell them to memorise the card on the bottom and put it back and shuffle the pack. Now again you can do many things or just tell them straight on.

Jumping rubber band

Effect: a rubber band is shown and put on two fingers. Then the magician closes his fingers and opens them and the rubber band has swapped places.

Method: put the rubber band on the two front fingers. Now get one end of the rubber band and pull it back. Put all four fingers in the loop and then open your hand and is should have jumped places. You can now wind another band on your top finger to give the proof you are not taking it off and putting it on again. Now with the wind band and the normal use two rubber bands and make them swap places. By making a loop for both of them and putting all the fingers in each loop. There are many different things you can do with this trick and they are all amazing.

I hope you enjoyed performing and amazing with these tricks. Remember to always practise again and again and again. That is the way magic works if you want to investigate further in magic look and magic shops or websites. Also remember to patter your audience to lean them away from what is happening. If you are doing something you don't want them to notice. Then do it quietly but if there are something you really want them to notice. Do it forcefully and make them notice it. If things go wrong then improvise for instance. In the coin changer if one coin flies off in one direction. Say that it is a bit early for it to jump and that the coin made a mistake.

Never ever ever tell your secrets because if everyone knew the trick then it would not be a trick. So never ever ever tell your secrets.

There are many things you can do with improvisation and sometimes it can be the heart of magic. So till next time (if there is one) good bye and remember to keeeeep practicing.

www.ingramcontent.com/pod-product-compliance
Ingram Content Group UK Ltd.
Pitfield, Milton Keynes, MK11 3LW, UK
UKHW020228250726
13967UKWH00001B/242